RESONANT RUBBISH

by
John A. Brune
Illustrated by Lilla Fox

Jaguar bone flute, British Guiana

THE ENGLISH FOLK DANCE AND SONG SOCIETY
Cecil Sharp House,
2 Regent's Park Road,
London, NW1 7AY.

Printed in England   © Copyright EFDSS 1974
I.S.B.N. 0 85418 097 4

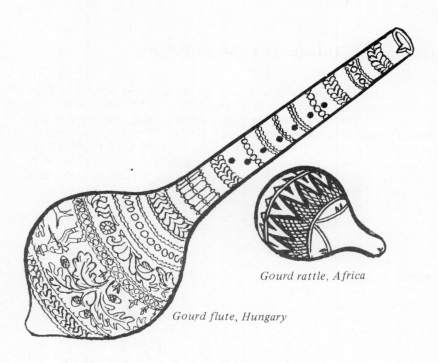

Gourd rattle, Africa

Gourd flute, Hungary

CONTENTS

MUSICAL INSTRUMENTS FROM RUBBISH?

An article that can be put to any use whatever is not rubbish. It only becomes rubbish if we lack the imagination or the enterprise to see and exploit its possible use. Early man, as far as we can judge, made good use of the vessels and containers provided by nature — such as shells, tortoise shells, gourds, nuts and bones. As well as for domestic purposes, he used them for personal adornment, religious ritual, and to make into musical instruments. Musical instruments were also occasionally made out of objects that initially served some other purpose, as, for instance, vessels and containers made from wood or clay. They were decorated and treasured as befitted objects resulting from so much labour. Some musical instruments were made from hollow sticks and logs — natural forms that had to be cut and hewn before they could 'speak'. The only instrument-making material that might have been classed as rubbish was bone made into flutes and pipes; but even of that we cannot be sure, as the bones so used might have been those of a sacred beast or bird, and their musical uses of a religious nature.

To such primitive people, and to those nearer in time, rubbish really meant rubbish — things broken beyond repair and all possibilities of use. Even within living memory, bottles, jars, boxes, paper bags and tins were frequently put aside in case they might come in handy — as they often did.

But in this Packaged Age, we are all sad profligates. Away we throw them:- bottles and jars of clear or amber-glowing glass — greatly to the public danger; fair paper, bright tin-foil, patterned wrappings and strong cardboard boxes; shining tins of all sizes; hosts of plastic containers — five gallon giants, homely wash-up squeezers, tiny bottles from the chemist's, elegant and shapely flasks and bottles from the bathroom — away we throw them to litter our countryside, float on over the oceans, block our drains, and cause grave problems to our refuse disposal authorities. How this mischief will end is, happily, not even remotely connected with our present subject . . .

As many a vexed parent knows already, some of our waste can be made to produce a good loud din when you bash it. Properly organized, it could produce a wide range of percussive sound, from a boom to a tinkle. It can produce a whistle call — just about — and, perhaps, a reed cry, or a crow — it all depends on the selection of hidden treasures that you find in your very own dustbin. You can use a gallon can as a big bass drum; but with a little more organisation, it can produce a gentle plucked string voice. By using it in this way you are merely following in the footsteps of generations of folk-instrument makers through the ages; but if you go about it with a basic knowledge of how sound is produced, you might well hit on something quite new.

3

The instruments actually described in these pages have all been made and used. Their voices have an affinity with the ancient and traditional music of the Far East. They can be used for fun; they can speak to the soul. However, they already exist. It is the instruments that have neither been described, nor, indeed, made, but have merely been hinted at, — those which suggest themselves to one or another ingenious reader of these pages — it is those instruments that will be the real bonus. To arrive at these new inspirations, it will be best to go through the theoretical chapter on 'Principles of Sound' first; — then, to build one or two of the instruments described in the practical section, and then to try and make some improvements on them — particularly in the tuning devices.

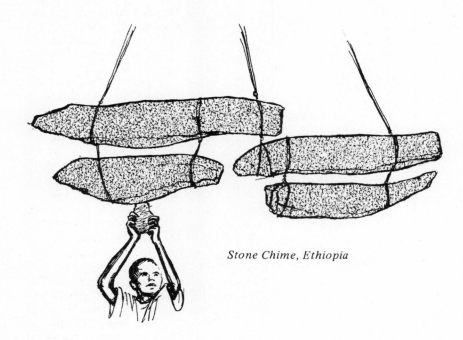

Stone Chime, Ethiopia

PRINCIPLES OF SOUND

Sound is the physical manifestation of vibrating air. Its pitch is determined by the number of vibrations — the frequency — per second. The lowest note on a piano has a frequency of about 30. The highest note has a frequency of about 4,000. Above and below those extremes the human ear scarcely registers the pitch of any note, and at a certain point the frequency becomes inaudible.

Practically any rigid material can be made to produce a musical sound. In altered form the same material can be made to absorb sound; for instance, a crystal-glass vase will yield a beautiful tone when struck — the frequency will depend on its size and on whether it is empty or partially filled with water — but if this vase were smashed up and ground into dust, it could be used for sound-proofing. Also, the same vase filled with sand instead of water would not vibrate either, but only make a clicking sound when struck. Water is, in fact, a good resonating material, conductor of sound, and a sound modifier that can be used to tune a vessel to a desired note. The more water is put into the vessel, the lower the sound will be when it is struck.

The sound of a musical note on an instrument is produced by some deliberate action, such as, beating, plucking, scraping, bowing or blowing upon a resonant material. This activated resonating material usually gives off a very weak sound on its own. So it must be amplified. The size of the amplifier is determined by the pitch of the activated resonating material — string, reed, column of air, etc.

In non-electronic instruments the amplifier is made of a resonant material, such as wood, bone or metal, which, in this particular shape, would be incapable of producing a musical sound on its own, but will not only amplify, but also modify, the tone-colour of the note produced by the activated resonating material. It is the amplifier of an instrument, rather than its activated resonant material — string etc., that determines the quality of the music produced. The same string gives off quite a different sound when stretched over a guitar, a banjo, or a three gallon can. That is why the amplifier, rather than the resonant material, is generally referred to as the 'Resonator'. Beyond a certain minimum standard the importance of quality in strings is almost marginal, the quality of the amplifier, on the other hand, is of prime importance. However, no music could be produced without the reaction of the string, reed or other resonating material to blowing, beating, plucking etc.

The more flexible a resonant material, the more versatile it is. A solid cube or sphere is accoustically dead. But if you elongate and flatten a solid cube into a slab. it will give off a musical sound when it is struck. However, it will give off only one particular note. If you wish it to yield a tone of different pitch, you will first have to alter its shape or its size.

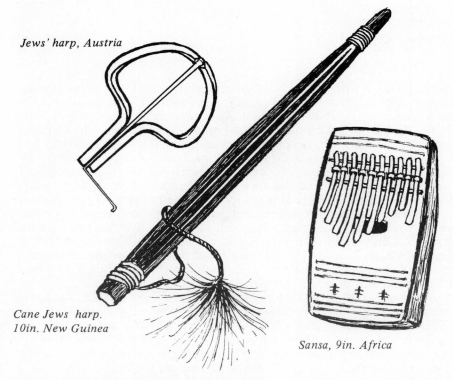

Jews' harp, Austria

Cane Jews harp.
10in. New Guinea

Sansa, 9in. Africa

If you keep on elongating and flattening your slab, you will eventually end up with a blade that will respond to plucking, if it is firmly held in a vice or a frame. The pitch of such a blade can be varied with the length that is allowed to vibrate freely. If you now pare this blade down into a tongue, or a lamella, and hammer or solder it into a frame to form a jews harp, you can make it yield a limited number of notes by using your mouth as a sound modifier and amplifier. Such a tongue, or lamella, on being plucked, will give off a composite sound, consisting of a bass-note and its various harmonics, that can each, in turn, be brought into prominence by the performer altering the shape of his mouth.

There is a limit beyond which a material cannot be thinned down and still give off a musical sound, unless it is stretched over a rigid frame or vessel. At this point it ceases to be a tongue, or lamella, and becomes a string or a wire. The musical scope of a stretched string is unlimited within a given range; any limitations there are within this range have to do with the structure of the instrument and the deliberate limits set by the instrument maker and the performer; — for instance, by placing frets on a finger-board.

Similar observations can be made in connection with shaped and flattened spheres, discs, gongs, bells, etc., that will each give off musical sounds. But the scope in this sequence is considerably less than in the cube-slab-blade-tongue-string range. It still goes through the various grades of rigid, semi-rigid and flexible resonant materials, but in its ultimate form it is neither a string nor a wire, but a skin or a foil in the shape of a circle. This can only be made to yield a musically useful sound if it is stretched over a frame or a vessel and becomes a drum, and even then it will normally only give off one sound when it is struck. However, it is capable of being tuned, and, provided the supporting structure is fashioned in a suitable shape, it can be made to yield a limited number of different sounds, of varying pitch. Such a stretched membrane can be regarded as a simulated rigid solid — (disc, slab, etc.)

Single membrane Shaman's drum, North America

Slit drum, Africa

Primitive pottery drum, Africa

The most flexible resonant material is the air we breathe. It is incapable of producing a sound on its own, normally. Even the wind is silent; it is the solid things, such as trees, walls and houses; the surface of the oceans; caves; overhead telegraph wires, and so forth, that make a storm reverberate with sound. Only in a hurricane or a typhoon can it be said that two currents of air, one hot, one cold, in head-on collision, twist and turn and roar before ever they strike down to the surface of the ocean or the land. For a useful accoustic purpose a controlled stream of air must be set in motion against a suitably shaped object. In this way it can be made to produce any desired tone in any pitch or volume. For instance, one solitary flute in an orchestra can sound above the entire string section.

Whether wind instruments can be incorporated into the scheme of rigid, semi-rigid and flexible materials is open to dispute. On the face of it they fall either into the class of rigid substances, activated by blowing instead of beating, etc., or, better still, they can be considered a cross between a rigid instrument and a reed, blade or tongue. In some cases there is an actual reed present, in others the reed is simulated by a compressed vibrating air-stream.

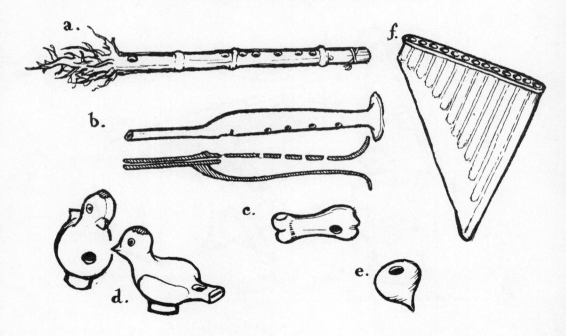

a. Sunflower stem side blown flute, Hungary
b. Pottery duct flute, Mexico
c. Reindeer footbone whistle, Stone-age.

d. Pottery bird whistle, Hungary
e. Fruit shell whistle, Brazil
f. Pottery pan-pipes, Ancient Peru

The sound of a wind instrument is produced by a controlled current of air vibrating in and around a tube, pipe or other cavity. Part of this hollow must be open, so that the musical sound produced can be projected into the atmosphere. The air in the hollow is generally referred to as a 'Column' or 'Body' of air. The pitch of the musical sound produced is dictated by the length and size of this column or body of air. The material and the bore of the instrument also determine the volume and the tone-colour. The inside bore of a wind instrument is sometimes cylindrical, that is, the same width throughout its length; or conical, — small at one end and gradually increasing in width to the other end. It may be partly the one and partly the other type. The tube or pipe may be straight or curved; open or stopped. Wind instruments fall into three classes:-

Free Air Reeds, *edge tones or flutes; (a)* where the breath-stream is made to vibrate against an edge in the mouth-hole on the upper side of the hollow body — usually a tube or a pipe. In the case of transverse flutes, piccolos etc., the breath is blown obliquely across an orifice near one end of the tube. This end is blocked. The rest of the tube is open at the other end, or at the first unstopped finger-hole. A miniature whirlwind is created inside the instrument to the length of the column of air, which is controlled by the player fingering the finger-holes or keys. Bottles, jugs, etc., of suitable shape and size, can be made to play in a similar way, but they will only produce one note and, sometimes, if overblown, its harmonic. In the case of a bottle, a musical sound is produced by the current passing over the mouth of the bottle drawing out the air inside; this is immediately replaced by more air being sucked in by the resulting vacuum.

(b) Other tubular flutes and whistles, and globular instruments like the ocarina, in which a flue directs the breath against the sharp edge of a sound-hole, through a channel in a beak-shaped mouth-piece. Most of these are blown vertically like recorders, penny-whistles, etc. Pitch is controlled as in traverse flutes.

Lip reeds trumpets and horns. The lips, slightly opened, are made to vibrate against a cup-or-cone-shaped mouth-piece. Their buzz is amplified in the throat of the mouth-piece, and modified by the size, the bore, the shape and the material of the tube. The quality of the tone depends on the shallowness or depth of the mouth-piece. The pitch depends on its size.

Cane reeds or reed pipes. The sound is produced by the vibrations of an actual reed, which can be of either cane or metal. There are three types of reeds, which are, *(a)* single reeds, that is, flat pieces of cane, shaved thin at one end. The thicker end is clamped to the flat side of a beak-shaped mouth-piece. Sound is produced when the player's breath causes the reed to vibrate against the mouth-piece. Pitch is controlled as in traverse flutes, by altering the length of the column of air at the finger-holes.

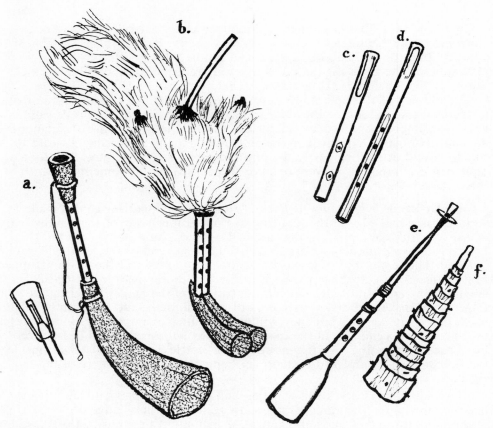

a. Hornpipe, Assam
b. Bagpipes, Tunisia
c. Single reed pipe, Cyprus
d. Single reed pipe, Ibiza
e. Double-reed shawm. Nigeria
f. Whithorn, England

(b) **Double reeds**. Two small pieces of cane of identical size and shape are shaved paper-thin at one end, and at the other, are bound together over a small metal tube, — the staple. The thin ends of the reeds are pressed together, leaving a minute gap between them. The lower part of the staple is covered in cork or like material, and fitted tightly into the top-end of the instrument. Again, the pitch is controlled as in traverse flutes.

(c) **Free reeds** — includes such instruments as the mouth organ and the accordion. The reeds are each tuned to one note only. They do not cause the vibration of a column of air, but act on the atmosphere at large, beating back and forth through a fitted opening in a chamber that merely acts as an amplifier.

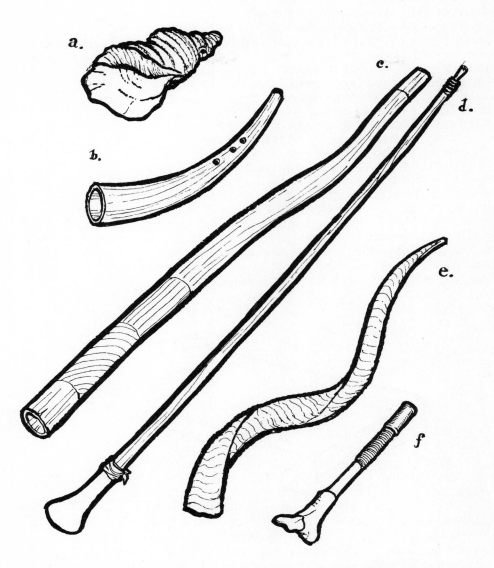

a. Side blown conch shell
b. Stopped cow horn, Scandinavia
c. Didgeridoo, Australia

d. Wooden trumpet with gourd bell, Assam
e. Goat horn. Zambia
f. Human thigh bone trumpet, Tibet

From the above run-down on the whole gamut of musical sound-producers it should be clear that an almost unlimited number of instruments in the percussion and concussion range can be created out of discarded cardboard boxes, plastic containers and tin cans. Also, a great many string instruments can be constructed from various plastic containers and plastic bottles of different sizes, fitted out with suitable necks.

With the inclusion of discarded glass among our resonant refuse and jingling junk, our scope for producing melodic and harmonic sound is vastly increased by the inclusion of crystallophones in our little band.

The real difficulties are likely to occur in the plucked reed and wind ranges. Here we would have to cheat and buy parts specially to make our disposables talk. We would also need a proper workshop.

In our examples we have concentrated on such instruments as can be put together in practically no time at all, with the minimum use of tools. For best results a drill is recommended -- but it is optional. However, a small assortment of tools and accessories is essential: a saw; a Stanley knife and blade, or a similar cutting tool; a rasp; a nail file; a hammer; some pointed implement for punching holes into tin and plastic, such as a dart; a long carpet needle; nails; staples; paper clips and fasteners; sandpaper; glue; dowelling; pieces of lath and battens; and Terylene fishing line. A bench hook, see diagram, would be a great help for sawing; it is much better than using a chair!

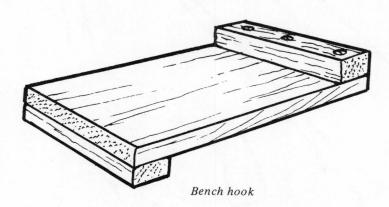

Bench hook

THE TREASURES OF THE TIP

1. *Plastic Containers* give a soft gentle tone, suitable for reflective music and to accompany solo singing and can be used for percussion and string instruments, the larger varieties with handles, also for concussion. When used for percussion, plastic containers and bottles can be tuned by being partially filled with water. With certain shapes, an ideal quantity of water can also be used for an additional gurgling sound effect, which is obtained by striking the container at a particular point at an angle. When used with string, all plastic containers and bottles produce a very similar sound, no matter how they are constructed. To get a different sound, one has to use an amplifier of a different material to stop the strings, or to build a hybrid plastic-and-tin instrument.

Plastic comes in a number of different shapes and sizes for experiment; it is easy to work; cuts like cheese; and is easy to make holes in and to decorate. Thinner and more rigid plastics are more resonant, but, at the same time, the containers have to be sturdy enough to keep their shape and, in the case of string instruments, to withstand the tension of the strings and to keep more or less in tune.

Some of the larger suitable plastic containers and bottles are among the everyday refuse of hospitals (for instance, their x-ray departments); also printers, and hardware stores; in fact, there are scores of industries using this type of can. For the smaller types you can cheat your dustbin or scrounge at your hairdressers, chemist's and from cafes.

2. *Tins* have a louder and sharper tone; a more restricted number of shapes; are harder to work. They have the virtue of sounding different from plastic and of being somewhat sturdier. They make good hybrid instruments with plastic containers or bottles. For tuning with a liquid, water is not recommended in tins; turps substitute or methylated spirit is ideal for tuning sealed tin cans.

Tins are mainly obtained from kitchen refuse, photographic suppliers, cafes, canteens etc.; gallon cans are not as common as they used to be but are still commonly used for liquids that would soften and dissolve plastics. They can be got at hardware stores, garages and fertiliser suppliers.

NECKS, FINGERBOARDS ETC.

For this, old broomsticks, handles of garden implements, bamboo sticks from feather-brushes, large wooden spoons and curtain rods etc., are envisaged, also odd lengths of thin lath and battens. But if you are in a hurry you can buy dowelling, and thin laths for finger boards. For frets on a flat finger board split matches can be used; on a round finger board, gut or nylon string can be tied round the neck to serve as frets. But generally unfretted instruments will be more manageable in our range.

STRINGS

Strings have to be bought; obviously, fiddle, guitar and other professionally made strings can be used — though some of those will be too strong for the instruments we have in mind. For certain sound effects rubber bands make quite satisfactory strings, though it is almost impossible to tune them. Where the string is not to be stopped — as on a harp — ordinary parcel string of the smoother kind will sometimes do; certainly, a lot of native African instruments, e.g. bow-harps, are merely strung up with any string at hand, without any noticeable ill-effect on the sound of the instrument.

But the best string for our purpose is Terylene bound fishing line, preferably old and already well stretched. This will slip at first, but after a while it will stabilise. (Nylon is unsatisfactory. It is altogether too slippery and unstable). Terylene is dear, at the time of writing, about £1.70 for 150 yards, but one reel will last a long while; also, it comes in various weights. It can be bought in sports shops.

Piano wire is not to be recommended. Only the thinnest is suitable at all, and even that needs a wooden frame or a dowel to take the tension. It is difficult to work with — even a loop is hard to make without a winder — and it is very prickly to the fingers. Also, any twist in the wire, that tightens up during tuning, will make the wire snap long before its potential tensile strength has been reached.

STRING-TUNING DEVICES

This is one of the difficulties if the instruments are made without proper workshop facilities; fitting fiddle-pegs, harp-keys or wooden pins for tuning, as on African bow-harps and Arab desert-lutes, requires a certain amount of precision, though not quite the fine precision one finds on a violin. Of the professional tuning devices that one can fit onto a 'junk-instrument' a guitar machine head screw and gear would appear to be the simplest.

Without workshop facilities a system of 'wedge-tuning' has to be adopted. The method is described further on in the book. The materials needed for making a tuning section are (depending on the instrument under construction) gut string, screw eyes or staples.

BRIDGES

Bridges, like some traditional religious feasts, come under two headings; movable and non-movable. For the movable type the best thing is a small plastic bottle, which will also serve the purpose of further amplifying the sound. On an instrument like a tray-zither each string has two such movable bottles. On a gallon-tin-ambicord or like instrument, only one movable bottle will be used for two strings.

Often a piece of wood or a piece of split bamboo will do as a non-movable bridge. This can be pinned or glued on if necessary, very often without noticeably affecting the tone. But there are better things to be found among our discarded treasures for bridges to our string instruments. The female kind of screw-on plastic bottle tops, turned upside down, and suitably nicked, make excellent bridges, as do the rigid plastic sort of hair curlers.

A long list of other possible bridges could be added but there is little point. We are dealing with waste materials, and each household will have a slightly different assortment. The only really useful thing that can be said in addition at this stage is that owing to the great variety of plastic shapes used as resonators, an assortment of possible bridges should be kept aside in a special box, particularly if a junk-band is being planned for a group.

SUMMARY OF TOOLS AND TREASURES

(a) **Tools:** Drill; Stanley knife; hand saw; rasp; nail file; dart; carpet needle; hammer; can opener (beer can and other type).

(b) **Accessories:** Nails; staples (the 'U'-nail type); screw-in eyes; paper clips and paper fasteners; sandpaper and glue.

(c) **Handles:** Broomsticks; handles of garden implements, etc., wooden spoons; discarded fishing rods; curtain rods; old umbrella handles and offcuts of dowels etc. as well as bamboo if available; twigs, sticks and wands; odd lengths of batten about 1in. x ½in. and 1in. x 1in. such as can be found lying about in a woodyard or on an old building or demolition site.

(d) **Bridges:** Small plastic bottles; bottle and container tops; plastic hair curlers.

(e) **String:** Any kind, but Terylene fishing line is recommended.

(f) **Resonators:** Anything fairly rigid made of tin, plastic or cardboard — disposable and discarded tins, boxes, plastic containers in all shapes and sizes; mustard glasses; non-returnable soft drink bottles, etc., petrol cans, lengths of metal tubing.

(g) **Mouth-piece for whistles:** Bamboo; plastic tubing (not very good); phials and pill dispensers from the chemist's.

(h) **Tuner for crystallophones:** Medicine dropper.

(i) **Foam rubber:** for ensuring close fitting, and for muting.

PROTOTYPES DESCRIBED

Percussion and Concussion Instruments

There must be hundreds, if not thousands, of instruments in the percussion and concussion ranges that can be made from waste. The noisiest things in this range are large tin cans and drums. The latter can be made into 'Steel Bands', which are musical instruments in their own right and require considerable skill to tune. From our point of view large plastic containers are more useful, as they can be tuned with water. Below a certain level, water does not affect the pitch; above that level it lowers the pitch. The maximum difference in pitch that can be obtained with water in one container is around one fifth below the pitch of the empty container. This is also roughly the tuning range that can be obtained from a set of mustard glasses of identical size. To get an octave or more from either containers or glasses, different sizes, or similar sizes of glasses or containers tuned to a different pitch, perhaps because their sides are thinner, will have to be added at either end of the set. In the middle of our percussion section of the band, we suggest that two or three tuned gallon plastic containers be fixed by their handles to a broomstick. With practice they can be made to produce a good imitation 'kettle-drum' sound. Containers with thin walls are more effective than containers with thick walls. For beaters, experiment with such things as sticks, plain or bound at one end with foam rubber to make a softer sound; wooden spoons; wire brushes; long plastic containers which will further amplify the sound. But for plastic containers the human hand is very effective — lower palm, fingertips and fingernails, also hitting with the container's own stopper.

Bouncing Drum-Rattle

Tools and materials: Knife or punch; hammer; staples; gallon tin or plastic container; broomstick; bedspring; plastic bottle; rice/seeds, etc., curtain rings.

Make a hole in the bottom of the tin, or plastic container, just big enough to force through a broomstick. If you have no metal cutter, mark the outline of the hole with punch holes: these can be broken into each other with an old screwdriver. The broomstick is passed through the length of the container which is fixed firmly to it about half way up, and with the spout on top. At the foot of the broomstick staple on the old bedspring. Next put some rice or other seeds into a plastic pint bottle with roughly the diameter of the broomstick at its open end, and also place some curtain rings round its neck. Fit the top of the broomstick into the bottleneck, line neck with foam rubber if it is too loose. This instrument is bounced up and down to the rhythm of the music; the container is beaten with a stick.

Tingling stick, Hungary

Bouncing Drum-rattle

Maraccas

Any long plastic or tin container convenient to the hand and with a stopper or top will do; Boots the chemists have an ideal one in their Hair Care department. Fill it with a handful of melon seeds/rice/peas/beans/nuts, either natural or metal, according to the sound you want; do not mix fillings as this results in a confused rattle. To prevent the filling from getting lost in the neck of the container, stuff this with foam rubber or tightly rolled paper.

Sistrum

A Comfort bottle is ideal for this, being ready shaped for the middle to be cut out with a knife or strong scissors. Make holes in the arms, facing each other, with a small punch or a dart, and insert one or two double-ended knitting needles on which are threaded a few curtain rings/metal nuts or washers. This will make a rattling sound. For a delicate musical jingle, pad the arms with adhesive foam rubber, bind the needle with the same, and use a multitude of those can-opening keys you see lying about on the pavement.

Lagerphone

Tools and materials: Hammer, punch, large-headed roofing nails, bottle tops, preferably with cork discs inside which can be taken out, doorstop or small piece of thick rubber, battens, 1in. x 1in., 1in. x ½in., or near, about 3ft. long.

This is a simple instrument, the modern Australian's version of the Aboriginal stamping stick with its jingling shells. Punch holes in the tops larger than the diameter of the nails; a folded newspaper makes a good surface to work on. Nail the tops on to the stick singly or in pairs, leaving them room to jingle. Nail the door stop or rubber on to the foot of the lagerphone, or the banging on the floor will drown the jingles.

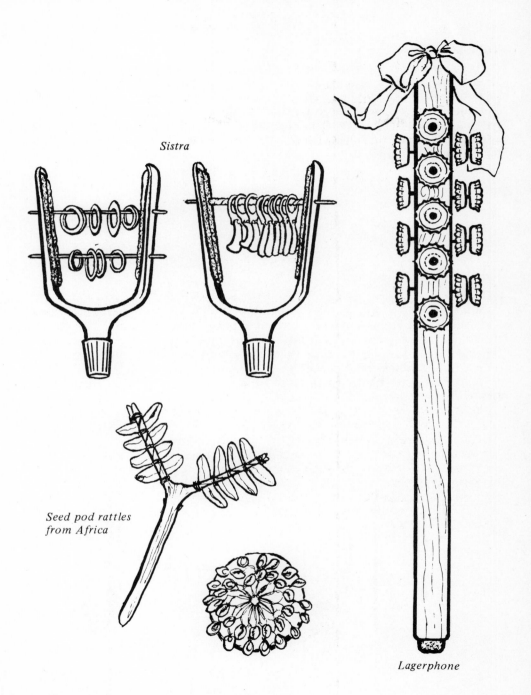

Sistra

*Seed pod rattles
from Africa*

Lagerphone

Tubular Bells

These are assembled from odd lengths of metal tubing suspended from a framework or a rod. Simple ties can be made as shown in the diagram or the suspending threads can be fixed on to the tubes with Sellotape or sticky paper. The tubes are beaten on the top nearside edge, and produce bell sounds. With patience, a good musical ear, enough metal tubing of the same weight, alloy and diameter, and a hacksaw, you can make a tuned chime. Here are sample measurements for a diatonic scale:

DOH	13¼in. or 33cm. 7mm.
RAY	12 $\frac{7}{16}$ in. or 31cm. 7mm.
ME	11 $\frac{5}{8}$ in. or 29cm. 6mm.
FAH	11 $\frac{7}{16}$ in. or 29cm.
SOH	10 $\frac{13}{16}$ in. or 27cm. 4mm.
LAH	10 $\frac{1}{8}$ in. or 25cm. 7mm.
TE	9 $\frac{7}{16}$ in. or 24cm. 1mm.
DOH	9 ¼ in. or 23cm. 6mm.

Some pottery flower pots give a pleasant chime when they are suspended and struck, but you are unlikely to find enough to make a scale. The same is true of bicycle bell tops, which can be fitted on to long nails or screws put through a board. Both these can be used as cymbals, as can the tin gongs on p. 26; but while you may obtain a satisfactory chime from a makeshift, you will not find a substitute for the true cymbal sound, as cymbals are very subtly and skilfully made.

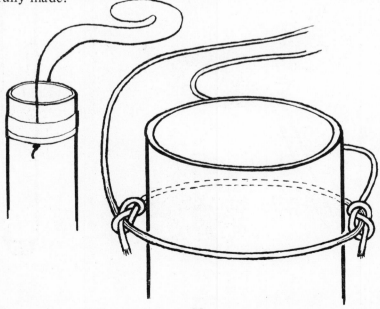

Tubular bells, showing two ways of suspending

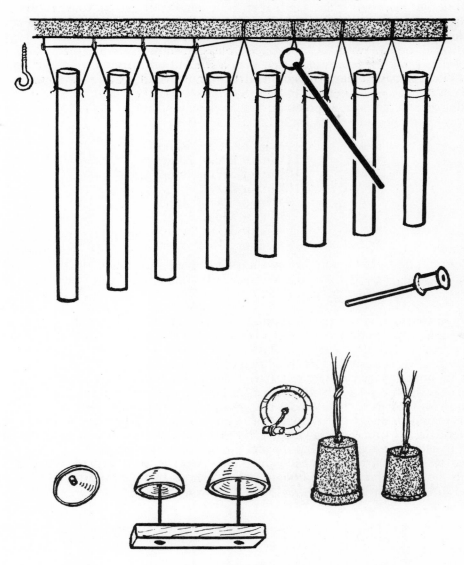

Bicycle bell and flower pot chimes

Wooden Xylophone

Tools and materials: Saw, sandpaper, rule, lengths of batten, foam rubber.

This is a familiar tuned percussion instrument, and many people will have made or played one at school. Ideally, the keys should be made from hardwood, but softwood will produce a pleasant musical sound if it is chosen carefully. Look for pieces of batten with a straight uniform grain and without knots or cracks; try them for sound with an improvised beater. Try to get enough of the same length of batten to make all your keys and then plane or sandpaper it as smooth as possible. The keys may be cut to the following approximate measurements for a diatonic scale.

DOH	12⅛ in. or 30cm. 8mm.
RAY	11½in. or 29cm. 2mm.
ME	10¾in. or 27cm. 3mm.
FAH	10¼in. or 26cm.
SOH	9⅝ in. or 24cm. 4mm.
LAH	9¼in. or 23cm. 5mm.
TE	8½in. or 21cm. 6mm.
DOH	8⅜ in. or 21cm. 2mm.

Add a note below and one above if you like.
12⅞ in or 32cm. 8mm.
7¾in. or 19cm. 7mm.

These measurements are approximate since variations in the grain of the wood may necessitate making some keys longer or shorter. To sharpen a key, saw a tiny length off the end: to flatten make a shallow cut across the underside. The narrow grains should be uppermost.

Sandpaper any sharp edges left after sawing, and polish the keys; this improves the tone. Lay them across a framework made of battens and padded with foam rubber; each key must rest on the framework at a point about ¼ of its length from the end. Squares of foam rubber stuck between each key will prevent them from knocking into each other when beaten. If you wish, drill a hole in each at one end so that a panel pin can hold it in place.

Beaters can be made from cane glued into wooden knobs or large wooden beads, both of which can be bought in Craft shops. Wooden spoons make a good substitute, as do cotton reels stuck on to pencils.

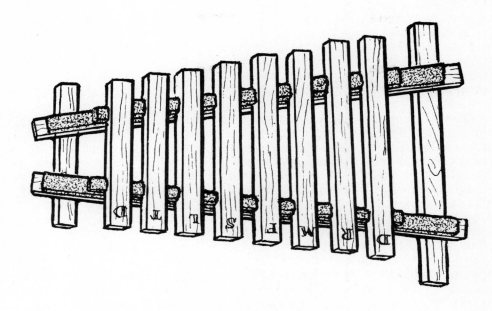

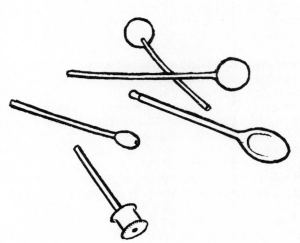

Xylophone and beaters

Crystallophone

The first thing is to take an assortment of glass jars, mustard pots, bottles etc., and stand them on a soft base. Hit each one of your assortment of discarded glass-ware with a plastic egg spoon in turn, to see which gives off the most beautiful musical sound. The selected vessel will be the type you will put aside for your crystallophone from then on. For our crystallophone we selected a particular make of mustard pot (Düsseldorfer Tafelsenf), which has a very pleasant timbre. Being small glasses, they give off notes of a fairly high frequency. For a lower frequency a larger vessel will be needed. As it is unlikely that you will have sufficient vessels of the selected type in stock for making your crystallophone, you will have time to look out for a base to stand your tuned glasses on. The size of your base will depend on the type of vessel that you have selected for the main part of your scale, and at this point it is well to remember that a number of glasses of a different size will have to be added to your instrument if a range above one fifth is required. If you wish to add extra low notes, a larger base will be needed, if you wish to add at the top of the scale, a smaller base will do. The base used for our crystallophone is a display stand thrown out by a general store. Similar stands appear, and are eventually discarded, all the time.

You now have your stand and sufficient vessels of the selected type to make a scale of five notes. Check whether each of your vessels gives off, more or less, the same note. If you are lucky, one or another of the 'identical' vessels will (for one reason or another) give off a note of higher, or lower, pitch than the rest. In our crystallophone one of the mustard glasses was a whole tone out on being struck. This gave us a range of one sixth from the chosen type of vessel. So, if we wish to extend the range to one octave and add a leading note at the bottom, we would have to add only three vessels of different size to our set.

The construction of a crystallophone is extremely simple. Arrange the vessels in a row on the stand, with any of lower pitch standing to the left, and any of higher pitch to the right. There must be a slight gap between the vessels. They must all stand on foam rubber and, if possible, lean against foam rubber at the back of the stand. Fill all of your glass vessels with water. This lowers their pitch by a fifth. The one to the extreme left remains full — about an eighth of an inch below the rim — the others will have their water level lowered with a medicine dropper. As you draw out the water from the second vessel from the left, keep sounding it and the one to the left until there is a semitone between them. This gives you the leading note and the tonic of your scale.

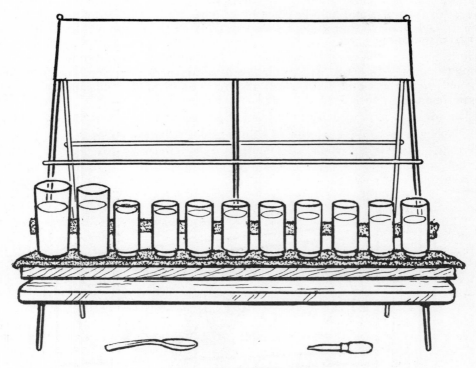

Crystallophone with beater and tuner

Your actual scale begins with the tuned second vessel from the left. The third vessel from the left will have to be tuned a full tone above the second vessel; — and so on, until you reach the octave to the right of your crystallophone — nine places up the scale. If you are satisfied with the range of a fifth, this instrument is not entirely useless, but it could rarely be used as the leading melody instrument, — only for the occasional simple harmonies. With enough glass vessels in a row it is possible to make up a crystallophone with a chromatic scale and a range of two-and-a-half octaves. This would have to be marked for water levels and pitch, probably with oil paint direct on the vessels.

Gong Chime

This needs an assortment of tin lids and shallow round tins, and a framework from which to suspend them. We used an old towel rail, but an expanding or a folding clothes airer would do, or a length of wood, its ends resting on two pieces of furniture and held in place by weights. Two holes are punched in the rim of each gong so that it can be suspended from the frame on strong fine string. This can be tied on to the frame or threaded through small eyes screwed into it, allowing the gong to swing freely. Generally speaking, the larger the gong the deeper the note, but pitch also depends on the depth of the gong and the nature of the metal, so you will have to experiment to build up your chime. Experiment also with hard and soft headed beaters.

Do not expect a musical sound from these instruments, since real gongs, like cymbals, are the product of highly skilled and complicated processes.

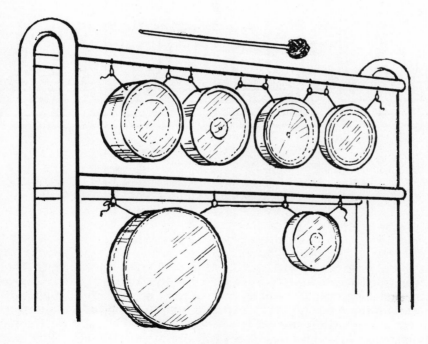

Gong chime

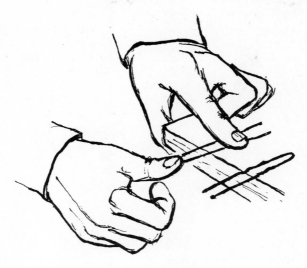

Plucked reeds (Try either end)

Plucked Reeds

The best plucked reeds are kirbigrips and wire hairpins; the thinner types have the best timbre. They are made to produce an African buzzing sound — like the bowl-lyre — by having a good bit of their vibrating 'free' end sounding against the table top. A big man with stubby fingers can get up to an octave out of one hairpin; a smaller person with thin fingers will get rather a shorter range. Place the open ends of your hairpin on the table and let the bend overlap the edge of the table; this is the plucking end. Next experiment to find the most effective position for producing the required sound on this particular hairpin. (No two hairpins are alike). Press your left index finger down on the open ends to produce your lowest note; keep pressing down as you pluck the bent end, and gently roll your finger to the right to go up the scale, and back to the left to go down. Another way of playing a hairpin is to tape the open ends down with Sellotape and produce the notes by moving the base of a typewriter-ribbon box up and down the scale. There may be improvements in technique — perhaps a sansa-type of instrument. Other reeds are Fruit-Ice lolly sticks, some plastic spoons, and thin metal corset bones.

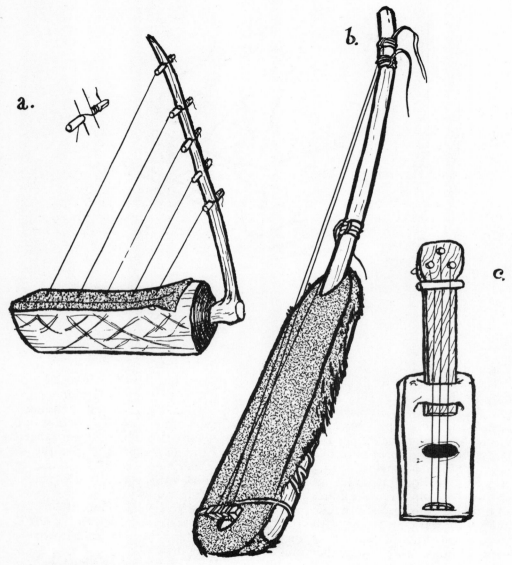

a. *Angle harp, Congo*
b. *Lute, Hansa people, Africa*
c. *Tin ramkie, South Africa bushman's version of European plucked instrument*

STRINGS

At this point we are getting away from the percussion range, and a few words on the classification of instruments might be helpful to anyone wishing to make a deeper study of some of the structure discussed.

Traditionally, instruments were divided into 'string', 'wind' and 'percussion'. In this classification there was no place for plucked reeds and a number of other odd basic instruments of folk music, such as those worked by friction, which would all have come under the heading 'percussion'. Hence all the types we have considered so far, including the 'hairpins', would belong to this section. On the other hand, a hammered string instrument would come under strings – if it is worked by hand – although it is as much a percussion instrument as a drum; but if it has a keyboard, it is placed in a group with other keyboard instruments – of which a piano is hammered, a harpsichord is plucked and an organ is most decidedly wind.

So, a more rational classification had to be worked out for the scientific study of musical instruments. The system was evolved by Curt Sachs and Erich von Hornborstel at the turn of the century. In it there are four main classes of instrument: 'Idiophones' – that is, instruments that are made of an inherently resonant material; 'Membranophones' or instruments whose sound is produced by beating, scraping or otherwise activating a stretched skin or other membrane; 'Aerophones' – wind instruments; and 'Cordophones' – string instruments. The system works tolerably well in spite of the fact that 'Idiophone' refers to the accoustic quality of a rigid or semi-rigid material, 'Aerophone' refers to a method by which sound is produced, and both 'Mebranophone' and 'Cordophone' refer to the forms in which a flexible material can be made to sound when it is stretched.

Hence the system is not all *that* scientific either. If ever any of our instruments find their way into a Museum, – however will they place a plastic container? – under 'Idiophones' or under 'Mebranophones'?

The four classes of instruments are subdivided into families, according to their structure or the principle by which sound is produced.

Cordophones fall into four main classes: 1. musical bows and harps; 2. lyres; 3. lutes; 4. zithers; each class being further subdivided. For our purpose we follow a simpler classification, based on the rigid objects that take the tension of the strings.

There are four kinds of string instruments:

1. Curved Sticks (musical bows and bow-harps, arched harps, etc.)
2. Straight Sticks (long lutes, short lutes, fiddles, guitars, angle harps, etc.)
3. Frames (lyres, frame harps, etc.)
4. Boxes (zithers, Appalachian Dulcimer, etc.)

This is a structural classification that does not tally with the normal grouping in each instance. For instance — bow harps, angle harps and frame harps are generally considered as developments away from the musical bow. On the other hand long lutes and short lutes still remain in the same group, even though their structure differs in some important details, and though their origins may be quite unconnected. A long lute is a straight stick with an amplifier (resonator) at one end and a tuning device at the other. The stick passes through the whole length of the amplifier and takes the whole tension of the string. In the short lute the stick ends where it meets the amplifier, and the tension of the string is taken equally by the body (usually the top deck or belly of the amplifier) and the stick (neck).

Whatever the true origin of any instrument may be, from the experimental point of view the basic structural differences are of more relevance than the superficial appearances and the apparent relationships one deducts from these superficial appearances.

All string instruments have a rigid structure over which a string or a number of strings can be stretched. Most of them have also an amplifier and all of them have tuning devices. Some frame and box instruments have more than seven strings that are meant to be played open; but in the case of instruments with fewer than seven strings some means of stopping them is generally employed. These considerations in conjunction with the structures described and listed above should indicate all the snags that are likely to arise when actually stringing up some flimsy discarded rubbish.

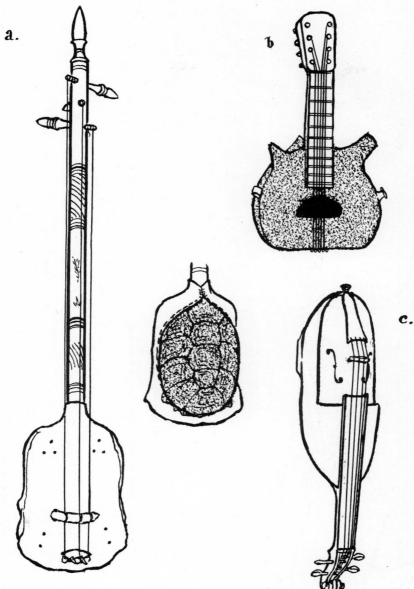

a. Tortoiseshell lute, Morocco
b. Plucked instrument made from leather bottle, France
c. Clog fiddle, France

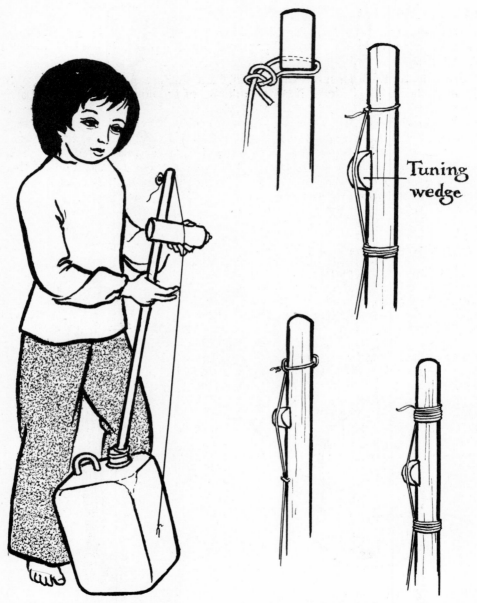

One string bass

Tuning
wedge

String attachment with tuning wedge

The One-String Bass

Tools and materials: A drill and bit; Stanley knife and blade; three to five gallon plastic container; batten; 4ft. x 1½in. dowel or broomstick; paper clip; length of string; staple.

Stick dowel through spout of container and pack it tight in the spout with foam rubber. Make a small slit into the belly of the container to slide in a paper-clip.

The dowel goes through the whole length of the container. The angle at which it is fixed will depend, as in every other plastic container instrument, on the shape of the container and on the length of the dowelling neck. If it fits too loosely, pack the container neck with foam rubber. It can be secured at the bottom of the container by a couple of tacks, which can also act as string holders when the container is flattish in shape.

Stringing and Tuning

There are several possible tuning devices: the simplest is the 'drill tuning-section', for which you must first drill a hole a little way down from the top of the dowel. When fixing the dowel into the spout, make sure that the drill-hole faces to the belly side of the instrument. To string up and tune with a 'drill tuning-section' you first fasten your length of string onto the smaller bend of the paper-clip, and slide the larger bend into the slit in the belly of the container. Take the string to the other side of the dowel, through the hole, and pull it tight; take it half-way round the dowel and keep it tight by holding it against the side of the dowel with one hand while tying a number of half hitches against the string, where it enters the hole, with the other hand. In other words, the string is doubled up against itself after passing through the hole. The string is then held close to the dowel about 2in. below the drill-hole, either by means of the staple that is hammered down leaving enough space between its arch and the dowel to allow the string to pass under it freely, − or it can be tied down with string or leather lace instead of being stapled. Tuning sections without drill-holes can be made by using three staples, or two lots of binding twine 2in. apart (see illustrations). To tune with a tuning section, all you have to do is to put any suitable wedges into the 2in. stretch to tighten the string.

Another method, used for the moroccan lute on page 31 is a round wedge fitted into a gouged hole. The hole is gouged in the neck with a suitably sized carpenters' gouge, so that one aperture is larger than the other. The round wedge, made from a narrow piece of dowel, a wooden skewer, or an old pencil, is tapered by hand so as to go right through the hole, and to tighten as it is turned in. The string is wound on the narrow end, the end of it being held in a slit in the wedge. Tuning pegs of stringed instruments such as fiddles and guitars are shaped with precision tools, but for hundreds of years the makers of many folk instruments have done without such tools.

Alternatively, screw a large screw eye a little way into the neck, tie the string to it with the string pulled as tight as you can, then tune by screwing in the eye. After a while, of course, the eye will go no further, and you have to start again; nevertheless, some people find this method the most satisfactory.

The string can be stopped by pressing it towards or away from the neck with a plastic container; it will lose most of its resonance if you use anything solid.

A good way of playing the plastic lute

One-string Plastic Lute

The construction of this is the same as that of the One-String Bass, the stick being a dowel or broomstick according to the neck of the amplifier, which is a suitably shaped plastic container or bottle. The instrument is strung up and a bridge slipped into place. The string is stopped by pressing it with a hollow object, which, like the hollow bridge, further amplifies the tone. The string stopper can be slid up and down the string: suitable string stoppers are: a short length of bamboo, small plastic bottle, hard plastic 'Sel de mer' box, small cardboard box etc. One end of all these should be left open.

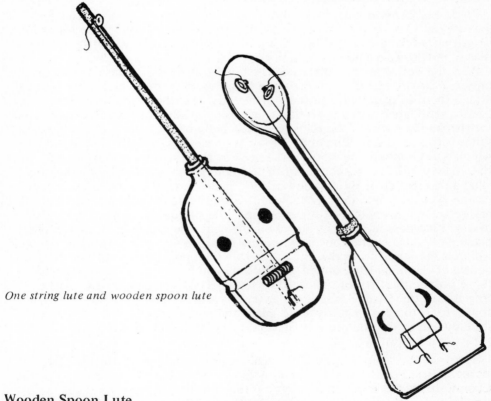

One string lute and wooden spoon lute

Wooden Spoon Lute

For this lute, a wooden spoon is pushed into the neck of a plastic bottle and wedged firmly with foam rubber. The strings, two or three, are attached to paper clips in the belly of the instrument, and tuned with eyes screwed into the bowl of the spoon. It is best played by sliding a small plastic bottle up and down the strings.

FRETTED LUTE

Plastic Lute with Fingerboard and Frets

Tools and materials: Hammer; knife; saw; tacks, two screws and screwdriver; screw eyes. Flattish plastic bottle; length of dowelling about three times the length of bottle; piece of thin lath about twice the length of bottle; small plastic bottle; Terylene line; match sticks.

Push the dowel to the bottom of the bottle, and tack it there; if you have only one or two strings, you may like to fix them to these tacks, but you can attach them to paper clips in the way already described. Screw the lath — it is best to sandpaper it first — so that it leaves about 2in. of the neck uncovered for the tuning eyes and overlaps on to the belly of the lute; it is bothersome to screw into round dowelling, but screws are necessary to hold the fingerboard which will be raised a little from the neck as the illustration makes clear. With the Stanley knife, cut a couple of little sound holes in the belly of the lute. Glue a matchstick at the top end of the fingerboard (the nut) and screw the tuning eyes into the sides of the head. String the instrument up, and slip the bridge under, this will need to be secured, the simplest way being by a 1 in. oval nail hammered into the dowel on the near side of the instrument. The placing of frets depends on the sounding lengths (the scale length) of the string which is measured from the nut to the touching point on the bridge. The octave of the open (unstopped) string is played by stopping halfway between those points; the fifth of the diatonic scale, SOH, is the third of the scale length, and the third, FAH, one quarter. Having established these points, you could, for a rough and ready scale, place the remaining points of the diatonic scale by ear, as did the old lute players, tying their frets on to the neck.

However, the scale length can be accurately divided into semitones by mathematics. For the first interval, divide the scale length by 17.835, for the second, divide the remaining length by this number, for the third, the remaining length, and so on. Originally, the dividing number was 18, which is simpler and quite accurate enough for a plastic lute. Indeed unless you have accurate calculating and measuring instruments, you may find the placing by ear the best way (after all fiddlers play in tune without frets). The frets are made from split match sticks and if you use a non-contact adhesive — such as Evostick wood glue, you can shift them about a bit before it dries.

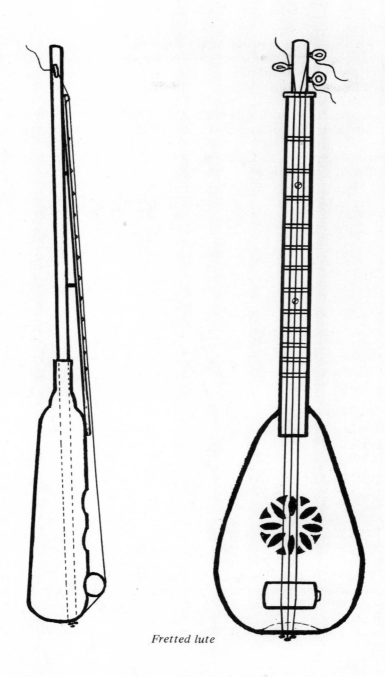

Fretted lute

Round Tin Banjo

Tools and materials: Punch or tin cutter; hammer and tacks; glue; shallow round tin, about 6 to 10in. diameter; piece of wood about 1in. by ½in. about four times the diameter of tin; thin lath about three times the diameter of tin; Terylene line; screw eyes; small plastic bottle; hair curler or screw on top; matchsticks.

Make a rectangular hole to fit the stick in the rim of the tin as near to the top as possible. Push the stick through and nail it to the opposite rim, using as many tacks as you want strings. Screw on the fingerboard, leaving about 2in. at the top for the tuning eyes, and glue on a matchstick nut. String the banjo, using the bridge of your choice.   This instrument may be fretted

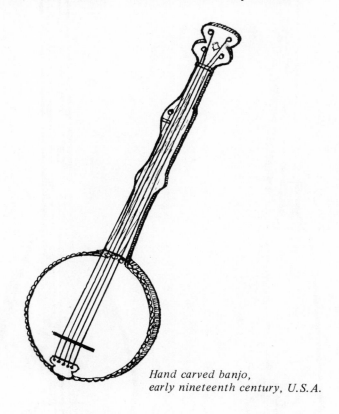

Hand carved banjo,
early nineteenth century, U.S.A.

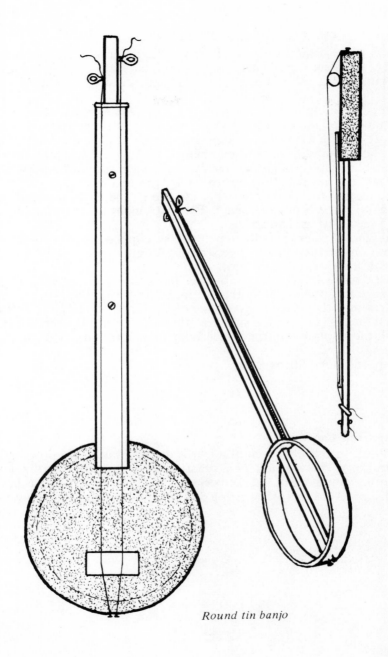

Round tin banjo

One-String Fruit Can Lute *(Chinese Fiddle Design)*

Tools and materials: A drill and bit; metal punch or piercer; hammer; Stanley knife and blade; beer can opener; empty fruit can with top removed; dowel 27in. x ⅝ in.; a 1in. paper clip; a 'female' plastic screw-top; a staple; a 1in. wire nail.

First prepare tuning section in the dowel (see 'One-String Bass').

Then punch enough of a hole into the side of the tin opposite the seam to be able to (just) wedge the stick through and force it against the seam on the other side. (The hole should be about 1cm. below the closed side of the tin.)

Drive the wire nail through the 'seamy side' of the tin into the dowel, leaving part of it and the head sticking out to serve as an end-pin.

Next, punch the top of the tin (what used to be the bottom when it was still a fruit can) with the beer-can opener. The instrument is now complete except for its end-piece, bridge and string.

The end-piece is the paper-clip which will be clipped on the end-pin when the string is put on the instrument. The string is fastened onto it with a 'figure-eight' knot. (see illustration).

The plastic screw-top serves as a bridge. The staple is driven through its top near one edge and parallel to it; about ¼in. is left sticking out on top. A deep groove is cut into the lower or open side of the screw-top away from the staple, and a small nick is cut into the side near the staple. Place the screw-top upside down with the staple-top in the punch-hole above the end-pin, with the deep groove nearest the end-pin.

String up. (See One-String Bass).

One-String Fruit Can Lyre

Punch a hole into the bottom of a fruit can and fit in a thin-dowel triangle (see illustration). This instrument is practically silent until the string is stopped by some other container (a 'sel de mer' square plastic container has been found particularly good for this). The string can be tightened and tuned with screw-eyes.

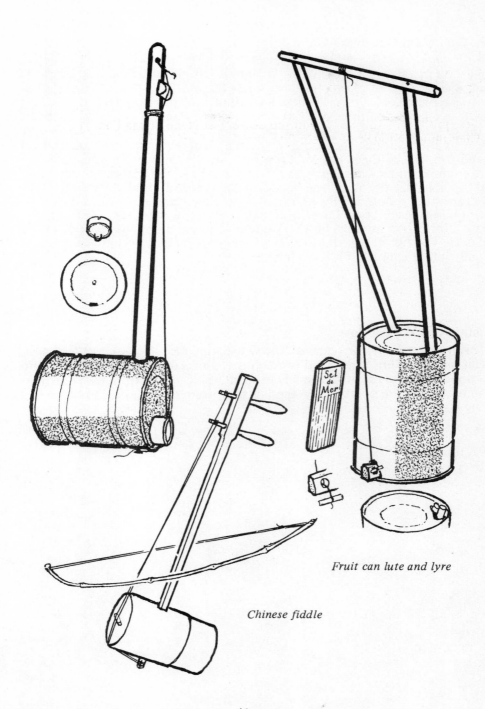

Fruit can lute and lyre

Chinese fiddle

The Gallon-Tin Dulcimer (Ambicord)

Tools and materials: Drill and bit; metal punch or piercer; a long needle; a one-gallon metal can; a broomstick; a pint or half pint plastic bottle (there are some square types of plastic bottles for less than half a pint supplied by some photographic chemical firms. These are suitable for our purpose).

Drill two holes at either end of the broomstick. Punch a hole into the bottom of the can immediately underneath the spout — just big enough to be able to force the stick through the length of the can. Securely bind the two strings at the bottom end of the stick, and draw both strings through the small plastic bottle (about an inch apart and about an inch above the bottom of the bottle) with the long needle. Stand the bottle on the top deck, that is the side of the tin nearest the spout, and fasten the strings to the other end of the stick into a 'drill tuning-section' (see 'One-String Bass'). Remove the screw-top from the plastic bottle, and turn the bottle upside down, with its spout standing on the top deck. Position the bottle so as to obtain the maximum length of string — roughly guitar length — on the plucking side.

Fishing Rod Musical Bow

This is structurally the same as 'The One-String Bass' etc., except that a discarded glass fibre fishing rod is used instead of a dowel. To play it, one holds the top-end of the rod with the left hand and plucks the string with the right. Different notes are obtained by bending and stretching the rod, and hence, the string.

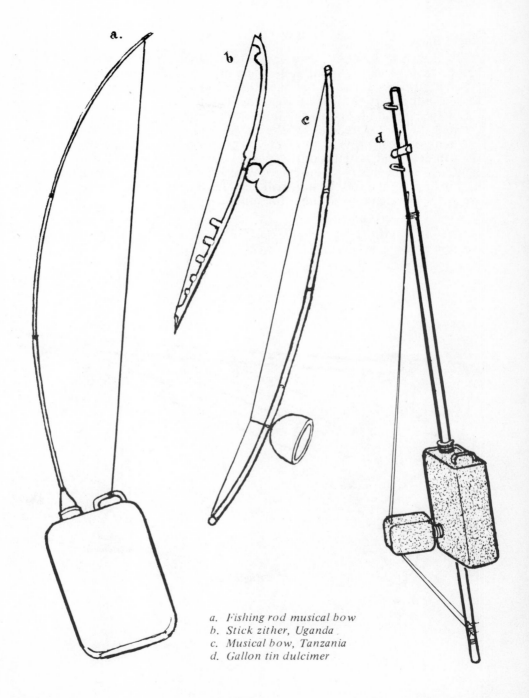

a. Fishing rod musical bow
b. Stick zither, Uganda
c. Musical bow, Tanzania
d. Gallon tin dulcimer

Angle Harp

The main parts for this are a one-gallon plastic container with a thick hollow handle that meets the spout at an angle on top, and a broomstick.

Cut a slit-cross at the end of the hollow handle away from the spout and force the broomstick right through the handle.

Cut two sound-holes into the sides of the container.

Punch five or seven holes for the strings into the top of the container.

When you string this instrument you first pass each string through its hole in the top deck and fasten it onto a paper-clip. The other ends of the strings are tightened by means of screw-eyes on the broomstick. If this instrument is meant to play in a folk band it will need harp keys or fiddle pegs, as screw-eyes are not very satisfactory things for tuning.

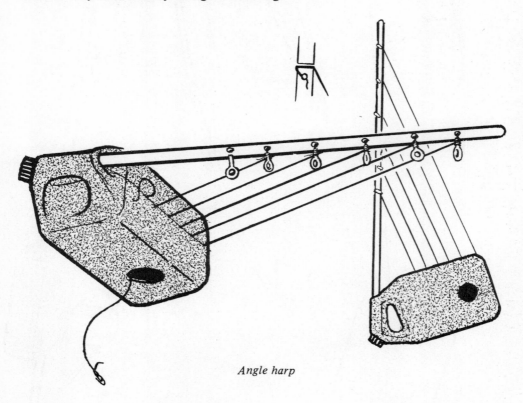

Angle harp

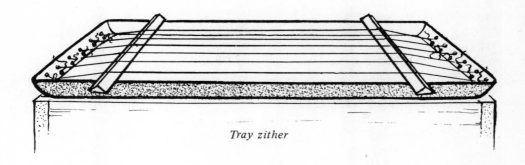

Tray zither

Trough zither, Uganda

Tray Zither

Take an old tray and bore holes (for as many strings as required) into the board at both ends across its length; a wooden or a plastic tray is to be preferred to a metal one. In the case of a metal tray, the holes will have to be lined so as not to cut into the string. Cut a small sound-hole into the middle of the tray. String up with Terylene fishing line.

At the tuning end of the tray there is a double row of holes. The string is passed through the inside hole first, drawn tight and held from the inside of the tray while it is taken through the outside hole, then it is held tight from the outside or back of the tray while it is fastened to itself with half hitches as on the tuning-section end of 'The One-String Bass' etc.; tuning is done by two movable bridges under each string.

The tray is placed over a box or a tin or plastic container with its top cut off. The strings are stopped in the same way as those on 'The One-String Bass', when required but are generally played open.

WIND INSTRUMENTS

Panpipes

The simplest wind instruments are end blown i.e. blown across. Bottles, jugs, keys and hollow tubes will produce a variety of single notes. Bamboo can be cut below the notches to make a series of end blown pipes; careful sawing is necessary as the wood is very hard and tends to split. Several pipes can be tied together with string in a row or a circle, the shorter the tube, the higher the note. Given patience, a good ear, and plenty of bamboo, one could make a scale. However, if only a few notes could be provided, say the tonic, the third and fifth (DOH, ME, SOH) they would provide a foundation for the band, the stringed instruments being tuned to them. The tone is sweet, clear and penetrating.

Mouthpiece for Block-Flute

Tools and Materials: A Stanley knife; A short piece of bamboo or hollow (tube, pipe or phial) section of suitable dimensions; shaped dowel.

Carve the two parts and fit them as shown on the illustrations. Then insert into a plastic tube/length of bamboo without knots in it/hollow stick/length of hose pipe etc. and make finger holes with a sharp penknife. The positioning of these holes to make a correct scale will take some experiment, so you will need plenty of spare tube or whatever you use.

We have given two samples, both peasant flutes. The Balkan flute is played with the sounding hole underneath.

Single and Double Reeds

These can be made from straws, reeds or the stalks of plants, in the same way as did the shepherd boys mentioned by Mersenne in his *Harmonie Universelle* of 1637. A tongue is cut from the stem below a notch, attached at either the lower or upper end; if the stem is of thick cane, reed, bamboo or wood, the point of attachment can be cut a little thinner to ensure movement. Or the tongue can be cut separately and bound to the opening in the stem. When the whole mouthpiece is taken into the mouth and blown, this tongue should vibrate to make a squeaky sound. For a double reed, the stem is carefully split and flattened to make a mouthpiece. Needless to say, the making and blowing of these primitive reeds is tricky and the results are noise-makers rather than instruments of music. (See the Whithorn made from coiled birch bark held together with thorns and sounded with a single reed mouthpiece, page 10).

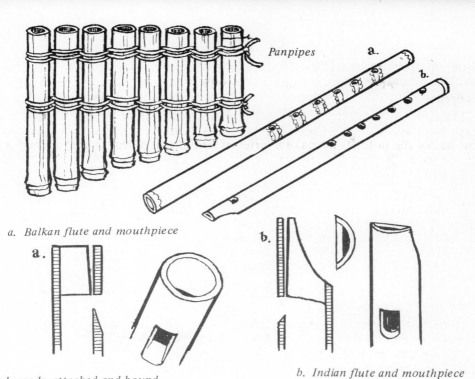

Panpipes

a.

b.

a. Balkan flute and mouthpiece

a.

b.

b. Indian flute and mouthpiece

Single reeds, attached and bound
a. upcut   b. downcut

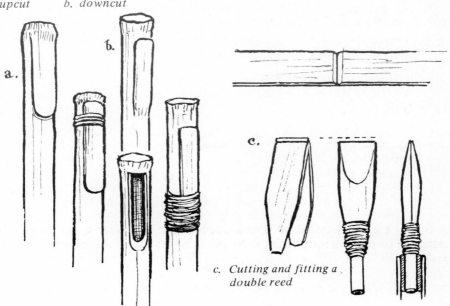

a.

b.

c.

c. Cutting and fitting a double reed

You may prefer to cheat by fixing whistle or reed mouthpiece into tubes or plastic or other containers with their ends cut off, in order to alter or amplify the sound. They must be wedged in very tightly, using foam rubber if necessary. The most effective music can be obtained by the use of the lip reed mouthpieces, those of trumpets, cornets or horns for instance. These can be fixed into a variety of common objects often found on rubbish heaps as well as in the home; such as watering cans, funnels, kettles, lengths of metal tubing or hose pipe or even the hollow parts of old bicycles. A number of harmonics can then be sounded in the usual way, by altering the tension of the lips: the longer the tube the greater the number of notes. You can also sing down these objects with quite startling results. By fitting tissue paper over the tops with a rubber band before singing down them, you will make them into mirlitons — voice modifiers, like comb and paper — and add a buzzing noise.

INDEX